MY DANCE WITH TIME

PHYLLIS B. PARUN

Copyright © 2022 PHYLLIS B. PARUN

All Rights Reserved. No part of this publication may be reproduced or transmitted in any means, electronic or mechanical, including photocopying, recording, or any information storage and retrieval system, without permission in writing. For permissions contact the author.

Permission to make copies of any part of this work should be submitted in email to
pbpstudio@yahoo.com

Cover art and all illustrations are solely owned by the author and require permissions.

Photograph Cover Design
and Illustrations by Phyllis Parun

EBook ISBN: 978-1-7323560-4-7

BERNARD PRESS
Publisher

New Orleans, Louisiana

First Edition

Dedication

Dedicated to all the people along my path
who have made mine a perfect life
by sharing their lives with me.

~

CONTENTS

I - Family
II – The Art Life
III - Political Baptism
IV - A Philosophical Quest

Epilogue
Acknowledgments
Author Biography
End Notes

~

"A life should leave deep tracks."
Ruth Ryan

I

Family

Inspiration
in life's winter
   this childhood

Great Grandfather Wolters Sr. and Grandfather Wolters Jr., both named Philipp, arrived in the United States from Hamburg, Germany in 1865. They lived for many years in uptown New Orleans near the Mississippi River. At the turn of the 20th century when Grandfather Philipp Jr. married Katherine Roth, they moved to a small town sixty miles north of New Orleans named Hammond.

Grandfather opened an upholstery and furniture repair shop in the front of their cottage. Grandfather and Grandmother Wolters had three daughters, Marie Philippine the oldest, Sophie Ada the middle girl and the youngest, Dorothea Catherine, my mother. As children, the three sisters, worked in the Wolters family shop, each developing different trade skills.

Broken chair seats
worn furniture
   nimble fingers

The elder daughter, my Godmother, Marie Philippine, became the family seamstress; cutting and sewing upholstery while the middle daughter, Sophie Ada caned chairs and learned bookkeeping. The youngest, my mother, Doris Catherine was the family artist who drew patterns or sketches needed. Her delicately shaded black ink, watercolor drawings and straight lines, drawn without a ruler attest to her fine eye and hand. As soon as I could hold a Crayola, my first drawing lessons, done under mother's tutelage, introduced me to the magic of line.

Who I am
deep understanding
Mother

In the mid-1940's while Father was stationed first in France then Japan, my younger brother and I lived with Mother's family, where as a young child I observed family members performing their furniture trades. Like mother, I too was an artist. But with little opportunity for an artist to earn a good living, my Aunt Marie made the practical suggestion that I develop a trade.

Four decades later, I too became an apprentice, carrying on the tradition of Grandfather and his daughters leading to the opening of my own Fine and Decorative Arts Studio in furniture restoration, objects conservation and gilding.

Treasure boxes
Grandfather's keys
what will they open

And there was music. An upright Victorian piano stood in the front room of our Hammond cottage. Mother and her sisters sang from an early age. In that house, there was always piano music, popular turn of the century sheet music, Vaudeville songs, Lutheran hymns, and later Jazz, boogie-woogie, and Rock and Roll.

In the 1920's these three fashionably dressed flappers, who copied designs directly from Vogue were very taken with New Orleans Dixieland Jazz, the Charleston and Southern Negro Spirituals. In the 1940s when Mother was pregnant with my brother and then diagnosed with breast cancer, her experience with pain and fear deepened her love of those Negro spirituals even more.

Singing continued into our teens with girl friends and neighbors in church, high school and carried over into my college years at Louisiana State University in New Orleans, where in 1960 I assemble thirty-five fellow singing students, founding the LSUNO Concert Choir - the forerunner inspiring the establishment of the college music department.

Lives of ancestors
reverberate
   a gentle breeze

When she reached 94 and convalescing at Poydras House in New Orleans, my Godmother-Aunt Marie confessed that all her life she really wanted to be a singer and her only regret was that she wasn't.

In her early 20's, my mother, a talented elementary school teacher, certified in the Spencerian handwriting technique and taught it to her students. When she married in 1938, the school system required that their female teachers resign from teaching to avoid exposing children to pregnant women - as if pregnancy was a disgrace. This sexism against my mother became fodder for my future political activism.

With no classes to teach, I became Mother's dutiful student, practicing for hours, holding my hand at a forty-five degree angle, penning lines up and down and ovals going round and round on the special paper lined with top, middle and bottom lines as guides for the penmanship exercises to fit precisely between them. Her lessons so improved my childhood block lettering hand, that my penmanship became almost as lovely as Mother's. In time, that beautifully trained hand sadly faded, having been replaced with an original scribble.

A heart filled with love
awakened me
    to the world

Mother died when I was 18. She was only 54. Her personal courage while suffering from cancer and the medical treatments, which eventually killed her, determined my fate

    The day she was passing, she called me to her bedside, took my hand in hers and squeezing it lovingly "good-bye" and with that was gone from me forever.

Moments so brief
so beautiful
  they could not last

Grandfather George Parun and his wife, Mana, our paternal grandmother and her first born, our father Bernardo, arrived in the U.S. from the small fishing village of Igrane, Croatia, Yugoslavia in 1913. Grandfather worked with many other men from Croatia in the oyster fields at the southern most tip of Louisiana. But soon Grandmother began to hate the isolation and lack of female companions so they moved up river to New Orleans. Here they opened an oyster sandwich store in the Marigny in the early 1920s where they sold oyster sandwiches, and food items as well as bootleg liquor, as did many in the era of prohibition.

It was told that one night Grandfather Parun got very drunk and hit his wife. Having learned boxing from Jesuit Priests at St. Aloysius Academy where he was schooled, Father was having none of it and knocked his father to the floor. Grandfather found this just cause to expel his son from the family home, causing Father to enlist in the U.S. Marines initiating Father's 20-year military career. After his discharge four years later, Father joined the Navy and when World War II broke out he enlisted in the U.S. Army.

With a sports and recreation background, our father was deployed to France in 1945 as Commander of the 13th Battalion Student Brigade for the American School in Biarritz, where he was, oddly enough, put in charge of troop off duty recreation activities. While stationed in France, he was promoted to the rank of Major and subsequently deployed to Kobe, Japan where his two supervising generals were Eisenhower and McArthur.

As a young child, I had no idea what my Father meant when he related the story that he told his "upper brass" he "would not execute any of McArthur's orders" fearing McArthur would get his men killed. Instead he would rewrite the battle orders himself in effect acting as his own general.

Behind
burned bridges
  fog ahead

It was 1962. The Vietnam War was on. As my younger brother turned 17 the draft threatened. Now retired our Army Major Father knew from experience what it took to survive war. He knew soldiers and that his son wasn't a fighter, commenting, "he would surely be killed." Deeply concerned, he set about to find a way to save his son from battle.

Off the front room of our home on Gentilly Boulevard, was a coat closet which Father had made into a small office by putting in a long narrow desk just big enough for a couple of pads of paper. That day he entered his office, pen in hand and closed the door to emerge several hours later with a fist of papers. Calling his son over, he announced that my brother should join the U.S. Air Force, which he calculated would just be entering the war four years later - the very year my brother would be discharged, thus avoiding both draft and battle.

My brother did just that and it turned out exactly that way. Father's World War II experience served him well. Stationed in Virginia for a year then on the Aleutian Islands for the remaining three years, my brother had avoided war.

Happy father
happy brother – both
   alive

A recreation educator and coach, Father taught both male and female students equally in his classrooms in the New Orleans Public Schools in the 1930's. At 14, I was one of the first females boxing and fencing - our family forte. At that young age and growing up in the 1950's, certainly no female liberation era, I did not really understand how odd it was for a female to be boxing and fencing. I thought of it as just another one of my father's fun recreational games.

Footprints ahead
too big to fill
   beware

Being part of a recreation-teacher-sports family, my brother and I grew up joyfully playing every sport and every game we could cram into our first fifteen years. My younger brother teammate, equally accomplished, always kept my competitive edge sharpened.

Born female
more brother than sister
   the two of us

While stationed in Japan after the US bombing, my father stockpiled cigarettes, which the devastated Japanese used as currency. Father took up smoking as well. The Japanese exchanged pottery, painted Sumi scrolls, hand carved sculpture, lacquer boxes and Chinese jade for cigarettes, which they needed more then their family heirlooms. Father would send these precious heirlooms to Mother who created a private Asian Museum in our family home.

Art, sculpture, painting
antique Asian artifacts
   childhood toys

While stationed on the Aleutian Islands, my brother had avoided the draft and spent the Vietnam War playing chess with fellow Air Force chess players - the best of fortunes.

After his Air Force discharge and his return home to New Orleans, my brother continued to perfect his game. Favoring speed chess, he won the prestigious title of "Louisiana Speed Chess Champion of 2009."

Brother's chess clock
always on time
   remembers too

When my brother died in 2014, I held an estate sale and sold an Air Force trunk I believed to be his. Five years later, an overlooked cabinet above the bedroom closet was discovered and opened. There his trunk was found, his name stenciled on it. Inside the trunk, were 8x10 black and white glossy photos of my brother and his buddies in uniform holding their chess trophies. On the same shelf were two large cardboard boxes with two-dozen of his chess trophies wrapped in now dry, brittle, crumbling 1975 newspaper.

I often wonder how many of that air corpsman he had personally taught to play in those three years.

Envelopes found
addressed in his hand
   silent requiem

On my twelfth birthday I announced to my father that I wanted to try a cigarette. Naturally he did not take lightly that his beautiful, healthy teenage daughter wanting a smoke.

Upon hearing my request, Father picked up a pack of unfiltered Camels from my uncle's desk drawer and turning to me with that unrehearsed manner so characteristic of him and said:

"Ok, but you don't want just one. I'll sit here and watch you smoke the whole pack."

Stunned, I coughed out "But—ah, --I only want one."

"Oh, no," Father retorted, "one is not enough. To experience smoking to its fullest, you must smoke the entire pack."

Needless to say, that this brief jaunt into smoking ended abruptly. And that was the last time I wanted a cigarette until long after his death.

Life lessons
live beyond
  the grave

When he was in his 80th year, my father's last wife died in Biloxi, Mississippi. That very day he and I walked along together between her daughter's house, where her body lay and her home they had shared for years, now his alone. With the same grief stricken face I had seen once before, he turned to me for comfort as he did that day my mother died.

"It is so difficult loosing a wife at my age," he sighed, shocking me back to that day Mother died.

"I don't think it is easy at any age," was all I could lovingly muster and that felt feeble, indeed.

Time passes
all things end
a joyful lament

A few years later, living in a quaint suburban house in Biloxi with caretakers, my father, the recreation coach, seeing a fellow housemate sitting on a sofa asked him,

"Why are you just sitting? Why don't you get up and walk around some?"

"The Doctor told me not to walk around," the man replied. Always in a teachable moment, Father had a ready response.

"If you don't start walking you will loose the ability to walk. So get up and we will walk around the pool table together."

Every day my father walked around that pool table. Some days he annoyed the staff by opening the locked back door to walk in the off limits back yard. Father was that "old dog' not learning those new tricks. He knew better.

No where to go
nothing more to do
   voilà!

After Father died I inherited his book collection as my brother had little interest in any book that wasn't about chess. Father's library was small, consisting of less than 50 books, unlike my enormous 3,000-book research library. How different we were in this regard. Of course, all of Father's were read and reread - and very potent ones they were too, sports, games, and philosophies of life, poetry, instructional manuals and personal conduct - while there are books in my library with spines yet to be cracked.

In the last years of his life, I remember his summation: *"Not bad for an immigrant boy."* He had always seemed so well assimilated that I had completely forgotten he was an immigrant - but he never had.

When Father died
time stopped – much later
  it started again

Father's most cherished book was a small black notebook of inspirational quotes. Its contents were sometimes handwritten while others were clippings from newspapers meticulously glued onto blank pages. Father carried this little black book of inspiration quotes with him throughout World War II from 1942 through to 1947, from First Lieutenant to Major in Kobe, Japan. This was his personal bible - these poets and writers - his priests.

Recreation athlete
Army Major - poetry
  his bridge

Aunt Mary, Father's sister, was born in New Orleans to their Yugoslav immigrant parents. Grandmother, Aunt Mary's mother named Mana, which also means "Mary" in Croatian, was Catholic.

When Mary died suddenly of a heart attack she left us all money. No one except her younger brother, our uncle and Father knew that she had any. They never said anything.

Mary grew a flower garden, never owned a car, never took a vacation in her 78 years then sealed herself in perpetuity into a tomb with her mother and father at St. Roch Cemetery never to be heard from again.

Many Christmases of gift giving past and she never said one word. She never tried to use money to impress us or to get us to like her. She just never said a thing. Oh--sometimes, I remember my father and she would argue about her not going on trips and spending some of it on herself. He would say, "You can't take it with you" so many times but this never phased Mary.

As her mother aged into her 90s, Mary cared for her elderly mother, single handedly for four years. She was the nurse, the bather, the hospice. And when I asked her how she changed the bed, she just said that she would roll grandma over, pull the sheet, put a clean one under her then roll her back onto it. She told us "taking care of my mother was the finest thing I have done in my life."

Mary was our aunt, our Catholic Aunt who walked every day four blocks to St. Peter and Paul Catholic Church to worship. She was our family Saint.

II

The Art Life

In 1951 Father was stationed in Camp Kilmer New Jersey after his discharge and return to the States. One day I brought a songbook home from school. Mother loved Southern Black Spirituals and "Swing Low Sweet Chariot" was one of her favorites. That song appeared in my songbook illustrated with a painting of the same name by Southern Regionalist painter John McCrady. It depicted Negro county life in Mississippi where McCrady was born and raised. When Mother noted that Mr. McCrady had his art school in New Orleans it was that very moment she decided that I would attend. Regardless of the cost and her cancer, Mother resolved to find the money somehow.

Go back in time
find today
   present

Upon our return to New Orleans from Camp Kilmer, Mother arranged for the two of us to visit John McCrady at his art school.

Upon ringing the bell, Mrs. McCrady, opened the dark green wooden gate door. We climbed a single file wood staircase, turned onto a veranda, and made our way to a narrow office at the top of the second floor just off the painting and drawing studio. I can still remember the odors of turpentine, oil paint and charcoal hanging from the rafters of that dusty old Bourbon Street building.

The World War II Veterans, my fellow students attending school on their veterans benefits, referred to him, affectionately as "Mr. Mac," but for a respectful young 15 year old that seemed a bit too familiar so he was always "Mr. McCrady" to me.

Rooms full of shapes
the sculptor's language
    came alive

Mr. McCrady was fond of having his beginning students draw studies for paintings in the French Quarter. On many a Saturday, he sent us into the French Quarter streets with drawing pad and charcoal pencils in hand to sketch. This was my first adventure into the Quarter. My mother trusted New Orleans and me to send her 15-year-old daughter home on the public city bus after school, something I would never do with a child of my own in today's New Orleans. New Orleans was a different city in the 1950's when this more innocent city was an exciting safe playground.

Longing for one fleeting moment
to return
　memories live here now

One Saturday morning, Mr. McCrady instructed me to begin a drawing from a still life set up in the large painting room. Each still life was changed regularly to provide variety. One particular day, I was drawing with colored charcoal from a display that included a green drape on the right side and on the left on a vertical pole hung a skeleton-like mask which was laughing with its jaw wide open and its hollow eyes seemingly staring backwards through time.

In the middle of that room was a long, flat, raised stage where a live model often posed for students to sketch. It was there Mr. McCrady regularly conducted group criticisms.

Students would prop their work in front of the model's large platform then sit in the folding chairs set out in front. McCrady sat first row center, students flanking both sides of him. He would observe each piece keenly, often in silence, and using a long wooden pointer resembling a pool stick, he would point to them making observations and suggestions about the work in front of him.

When McCrady reached my charcoal drawing, he just looked at it, contemplating in silence. Finally, he said, "That mask is laughing like it is laughing at Death." Then he repeated himself. That was all he said. I did not know at the time that Mr. McCrady had cancer, as did my mother of which both would eventually die years later.

All that is left of that drawing now is a Kodachrome slide and the $5 easel on which the study was done, a gift from my father, still in my studio these many years later.

Stare at time it slows
sometimes stopping -
   haunting

For inspiration, on my 16th birthday, my parents gave me the first edition of Janson's <u>The Picture History of Painting</u>. That was the beginning of classical art and many aesthetic love affairs.

First art book
Michelangelo's women
   half male

Drawing and sculpture were my first loves with photography the third. I spent years snapping pictures with various cameras. After nearly 50 years of looking through lenses, my studio is now filled with several thousand negatives from those celluloid years.

It all began with family photos snapped by my mother, her sisters and friends with their Kodak Brownie box cameras then later a Polaroid and 8 mm film. They were very gifted in staging and framing pictures those spontaneous photos and even as a naïve child I could see that their craft was inspired by European painting and sculpture which I eventually came to love.

When I bought a Nikkormat in 1976, the pictures I snapped were every subject. My first photographic mentor was my Aunt Sophie, our family photo-archivist. When Aunt Sophie departed this life at the grand age of 92, she left behind a legacy of 2,000 slides and photographs along with 20 reels of 8mm and Super 8 film with one simple message: "Time passes so take the picture".

All things perish
beauty lingers
   forever longing

III

Political Baptism

It is often said that one's early family life sets the stage for what one will become later in life, while one's accumulated life experience hones personal beliefs, character and life perspective.

The bus ride

One Saturday afternoon after art class at John McCrady's Art School, I took the bus home from the French Quarter, as I had many times that summer. But this time was different. Upon entering the bus, I was once again presented with the same two seating options: sit in front of the 'Colored Only" sign or sit behind it. I sat behind it.　It was 1956. I was 15.

A white sitting behind the "Colored Only" sign was strictly verboten. That day the bus stopped. The driver left his seat and came over to tell me to "sit in front of that sign or "the bus wasn't moving" until I did.　I didn't.　When that driver saw that I wasn't budging, he moved the sign behind me then returned to the driver's seat and drove on.

I have no recollection of ever hearing the name of Rosa Parks, the black woman who refused to move behind the sign in 1955, but on that day I too was over it. There was one huge difference, however. When Rosa Parks refused to move to the back of the bus she was arrested but when a little 15-year-old white girl refused to move to the front of the bus there was no arrest. My protest seemed ineffective as the driver continued on as he always had. Over many years I have learned of many of my Caucasian contemporaries who also refused to move in front of the sign in protest of racist seating. None of us removed as Rosa Parks was.

When I began college in 1959 as an idealistic student barely 18 and just out of high school, not being academically inclined, I felt undereducated compared to my smarter contemporaries. I thought that a college education would catch me up to everyone else. After extensive studies in rationalism and Aristotelian logic, I naively believed these tools would surely solve all human problems and create a better future civilization. And I thought everyone else also thought so. But in these subsequent seventy years, history has not proven this to be true.

While philosophical studies had trained me in logical thinking, I failed to grasp the truth that logic alone would not save the human race from itself. To my surprise, it turned out that my college education had put me ahead of the crowd. In retrospect, I see that logical thinking was never going to be a populist approach or even the ideal solution to the problems humanity faced.

Having studied the life of Socrates, I should have realized the fallacy in that thinking!

The one day when I asked my speed chess champion brother about how one plays the game of chess, which is a game of strategy, albeit military strategy, his answered was simple.

"There were two ways to play chess: by using mathematical logic or by using force, "a good player has to use both."

That was the missing piece: when logic is not a winning strategy, power plays are necessary.

The Working Life

After graduation, I sought employment in any job I could find. But jobs for educated women were scarce. We were not wanted. It was commonplace for interviewers to say that we were "overqualified" even if we could do the job easily. Even my application for a factory job and UPS driver was rejected. To use a phrase my Father often quoted: Life was "about to test my metal."

Trying to find my footing in the working world, I took various odd jobs. Initially, it was as a newspaper copy editor - a job my aunt Sophie had done in the late 1920s. Mine was at a small local Jewish press. I hated editing, as it was unimaginative so when I proved to be very bad at it, I was quickly let go.

Then there was the job in the medical records room at Touro Infirmary where I filed medical folders, which was much like my experience working in the college library. It was an easy one though not much of an intellectual challenge. And I worked in a dungeon of a basement room with no windows for eight hours a day. This quickly became a very dismal experience.

Libraries, however, were an easy choice for me since that was my student job as an undergraduate. So I made the rounds working at the New Orleans Public Library, Loyola University, Tulane University and the New Orleans Public Library. Library jobs were by far my favorite since I loved books and learning so libraries suited me very well. The library atmosphere was quiet and the work meditative. It was the perfect fit.

There are fantastic tales in the many jobs I held - all influencing my personal development and life direction. One job in particular comes to mind. It was when I worked at the YMCA as an Adult Education Instructor in 1964.

I was hired to teach college education classes designed to improve student performance on the college entrance exam. It was while there that I met the director who was putting himself through medical school and who would later hired me as a receptionist in the first abortion clinic in New Orleans. At the YMCA, I was tasked with helping clients complete the intake paperwork and much later was able to avail myself of its medical services the one time I needed them.

In those days in the 1960s, the rapid home pregnancy testing kit was readily available whereas birth control pills were not yet developed and the morning after pill was just a dream. As a result almost all women came to the clinic when they were merely 8-10 weeks pregnant, thereby, making for the simplest procedure, the D&C.

Graduate school at Louisiana State University in Baton Rouge was a life lesson in sexism, which I had not encountered while in undergraduate school. In those days, it was commonplace that one of the unspoken prerequisites for graduation for female graduate students included having sex with the thesis advisor. While some of my female colleagues in other graduate schools submitted to this heinous practice, when one of my professors approached me, I refused. However justified, my refusal was met with serious consequences to my professional teaching career.

Even though my transcript showed a "successful completion" of the Masters Thesis, the Chairman of the Philosophy Department refused to confer the degree, falsely claiming that I was "not qualified." He made this claim in spite of my having completed the requisite eight graduate courses and earning two A's in courses taught him - that very same department chair who had declared me to be "unqualified." Did he ever read Aristotle or study logic? What a dim wit!

In this atrocious situation, I was not alone. There was another female student in the Philosophy Department that year subjected to this same egregious sexist practice. Both of us refused to comply and both of our degrees were denied. She, however, did not appeal so I was left to be the tall nail to get hammered.

What you need to know, dear reader, in order to understand the situation, is that when a student entered this graduate school we did so under a catalogue which prescribed eight years to complete all requirements including all classes, a graduate thesis and also any appeal. Having completed all of these requirements and still refused graduation, I took the final step and appealed the decision within the required eight years by hiring a female attorney who claimed to be an equal rights attorney.

The hearing was conducted at the main campus in Baton Rouge with both the Philosophy Department Chair and the Graduate Division Chair in attendance. During this hearing, instead of addressing the terms of my appeal based on my having completed all the catalog requirements, the Chairman of the Philosophy Department stopped the appeal process and turned to the outgoing Chair of the Graduate School requesting and receiving a dismissal of the eight-year rule, effectively invalidating my appeal. Was that even legal?

Raising no objection, my attorney was feebly silent at this sideways administrative maneuver. After my appeal was denied, when I requested further court action be taken, she declined to put the case before the Louisiana Supreme Court, for reasons of her own. This appeared to me to be a simple lack of guts and commitment to the cause of fighting for female student rights and justice. She was no Gloria Allred!

Can you imagine my rage! I had been a victim of sexism, an injury compounded by the betrayal of a female attorney claiming to defend women's rights. All I could feel was that any hope I had to fulfill my deceased mother's dream for me to become a college professor was thwarted a that hearing.

But as it turns out, this was only the beginning of a longer journey. I was not about to let this setback foil me. The social and political climate of these late 1960s were just the fodder needed by the fermenting feminist equal rights movement and when it came, I was definitely in.

Out of the womb
Full strident woman
Hammered by patriarchy
Standing tall
Sweet revenge

Just twenty-five and still looking for a good job, in 1966, I entered The Charity Hospital School of Nursing as an Operating Room Technician who assisted surgeons by handing instruments to them. I enjoyed anatomy and Operating Room Technology (OR Tech). I found this job exciting, and looked forward to every day. But the enjoyment was quickly overshadowed by the gender and racial injustice, which I encountered every day working in that hospital. It was impossible for me to turn a blind eye to the abhorrent practices I witnessed. All sorts of injustices occurred in those operating rooms. So I reported each one of them to the hospital ombudsman. Working there we worked in the gender and race wars prevalent in that decade.

There was the white surgeon who one day announced that he was going to refuse plastic surgery to a 15 year old black teenager who had burned over 55% of her body in a house fire merely because he did not like that her mother hired an attorney to secure her daughter's surgery.

Then there was the male doctor who called a woman "fat" in front of the attending staff when he thought the patient was completely anesthetized and could not hear him. And in another operating room incident yet another white male surgeon refused to allow the female anesthesiologist to administer additional anesthesia to a female patient as he sadistically removed a breast tumor while she screamed in pain. This was enough to make every one of the women in that OR want to throw the surgical instruments at him. This incident would never happened during any surgery that involved male genitalia, you can be sure.

When my reporting came to the attention of our program director, a World War II seasoned nurse who was tough as nails after working under war conditions, she called me into her office to say that she had told us "that this job was not going to be easy and that some of us would not be able to take it." Mistaking my propensity for social reform as a lack of grit, she laid me off. That was just the beginning of my radical awakening.

Civil Liberties

As I sat in the hallway waiting for my pink slip to officially lay me off, a black female senior OR Tech approached me.

"What are you doing?" she reproach, "Waiting for your pink slip? Then what? Are you going to get an attorney to fight for you?"

"Well, yes, I thought I would call ACLU," I said.

"Look, let me tell you that twenty years ago I was fired too and in the very position you are in today but I refused to leave the job telling them they would just have to arrest me and if they did I would go to the press. Since they did not want negative publicity they didn't follow through and I kept my job. And I'm still here twenty years later. If you leave now this will be the end of your appeal. It won't go anywhere and you will be out of a job."

I really got what she meant and grateful she spoke up. Here was a black woman who had fought hard to stay on her job because she wanted and needed it. But the truth was that I just didn't have her guts, and I did not feel that this job was for me. My destiny lay elsewhere.

It turned out she was absolutely right about the outcome. ACLU failed to settle the complaint and I was never reinstated or compensated. But, as I look back on those years, all was not lost. That same ACLU attorney was revisited in 1976 when I worked for the New Orleans Public Library as the Visual Arts Coordinator for the Artists Information Bureau. It was then that ACLU was able to win a landmark first amendment ruling for artists. But that's another story for later.

None of these incidents shook my commitment to civil liberties as I continued down the road opening in front of me.

In 1968, I was hired by the director of the New Orleans Urban League as one of two "token whites" on the staff. The position paid better than any I had had prior. It was one of President Johnson's "War on Poverty" federally funded training programs intended to put more blacks into the workforce.

Everyday I would drive my VW bug into a black neighborhood on Desire Street to a Baptist church where classes were held for local black residents. The attendees received federal stipends to attend these job-training classes five days a week. It was our mission as Urban League staffers to simulate job interviews, teaching proper corporate workplace business attire, speech and etiquette, which were supposed to help blacks become upwardly mobile.

This War on Poverty program failed miserably for any number of reasons the least of which was there were paltry few jobs for the unskilled and particularly for blacks in the workforce. So the program resulted in a one year of a temporary job for the attendees.

But the war on women continued. And it was while at The Urban League that I was raped by a staff member, a former Black Panther who later bragged that it was his personal agenda to "impregnate as many white girls as he could apparently as part of a strategy to increase the black population. Thanks to birth control pills his mission was thwarted.

Teaching

The one time I did get a college teaching post it was at a black university. I joined the freshman faculty at Dillard University in the fall of 1968. This was a federally funded experimental teaching program intended to raise the education level of black students. This was an appointment that I loved and for which I was well prepared to pull out all the stops.

The federal grant, which Dillard received, was only for one year. It was an experimental education program and with little room for traditional teaching. The freshman students entered having tested with 4th grade reading skills and the faculty was charged with bringing the student grade point level up as high as we could in one year. To do this we used very unconventional methods.

Our methods were very unconventional. We used anything we found effective. Some of the white faculty used poetry and reading novels. I used philosophy, math and art. Sometimes we took them on civic educational tours of state prison and mental healthy facilities then asked them to write essays about the experience. That one-year the students jumped four grades in reading skills – a remarkable feat for just mine months.

The faculty meetings were another unconventional story. As white members of the faculty, the Black teachers trounced us weekly for what they called our "liberal teaching methods" which they deemed "a worthless liberal education which would not get black students into the middle class."

Of course, this was not our intention as we truly sought to liberate them from what we had experienced as a white patriarchal colonialists educational system that was turning out clones to conform to rather then teaching students to think for themselves.

It was, after all, the late 1960s, the era of anti-Vietnam protests, civil liberties for blacks, women and gay. Many of the black instructors largely felt that for Black Americans to survive in a white world, the students needed to be better than "whitey" at their own game. Though we also supported that point of view, many of us whites had had the experience that even whites couldn't survive patriarchy without some kind of edge. We sought to teach that edge. All faculty members had valid points.

Often faculty meetings were hotbeds of political disagreements. One Black female teacher, we will name Claudia G., consistently blasted me for using art and philosophy as part of my teaching-reading methods. There were three white liberals on the faculty, a male named David L. from UCLA whose Japanese grandparents were in US concentration camps during World War II, and a female S.H. from an upstate Ivy League college and me, a New Orleans born female who felt fortunate to able to get a college education at a newly opened state university.

When teaching English, David L. had students write poetry just the way they spoke – certainly iconoclastic for the day. Over the course of the year the students learned to write standard American English better as they learned the differences between the dialects they spoke and standard American English they were expect to learn. His approach was really very clever and proved to improve both their writing and reading skills.

When Claudia G. a fellow New Orleanian, got engaged the other white female on the faculty, Sandra H., a white Jewish woman from Philly, gave her a shower and did not invite me. When the shower convened, Claudia G. asked where I was. Sandra H., the hostess replied "Well, I thought that you did not like Phyllis since you two disagreed so often at faculty meetings. So I did not invite her."

Claudia G., also a New Orleanian born and educated teacher, was outraged. "Just because we disagree doesn't mean we don't like each other or that we are not friends."

How true. Sometime the best of friends and family are passionate about important issues and so it was with us. I did receive an apology from that upstate faculty member who admitted she had just taken our banter the wrong way.

While at the Urban League, I had asked another fellow staff member, one of the elder black men, another New Orleanian, why he remained in New Orleans so long. His reply was revealing: "New Orleans is like one big dysfunctional family. Can't live with them and can't live without them. I just stayed here."

And so it was with the faculty at Dillard that year. We each enjoyed the political debates and the dialogue about the best way to educate black students so they could economically and socially advance. And we gave it our all. Sometimes there were deep disagreements between us native New Orleanians and as Claudia G. pointed out to the northern faculty member from Philly, we were "still family here." This respectful banter and hashing out different political views was just not in that Philly gal's experience. From her northern chauvinistic perspective she must have thought that the southerners were having a race war when we really were just rapping out our views.

A Harvard Summer

One of the perks of teaching at Dillard that year was a summer scholarship to Harvard University. That summer of 1969 was set in a climate of social protest, sexual experimentation and political unrest. It was the summer of Woodstock, the New York Stonewall Riots and police in riot gear face off with hippies on the Cambridge Commons.

While at Harvard I was immersed in the burgeoning mental health reform movement, and able to study social sciences with cutting edge professors from Ivy League Universities from Harvard and Stanford at the peak of the decade in an era of the psychology pioneers Abraham Maslow, Carl Rogers, and T.D. Suzuki.

It was the summer I attended a Janice Joplin concert at Tanglewood with another Harvard summer student, a female, who was unabashedly flirting with me even though she was for all I knew heterosexual and married to a man. Yes, you guessed it, her flirtations led to a one-night stand after the concert. It was that kind of summer.

I remember sitting high in the bleaches with a clear view of the entire stage. The concert did not start on time after a hour passed with no sign of Joplin, I got antsy and felt like leaving but my companion urged me to stay and wait until it was "officially" cancelled. But it never was. Two hours passed. Surely, that was a cancellation. But no, they announced "she was on her way out momentarily.' Later we learned that the cause of the delay was that she was stoned on heroin and needed to pull herself together. Eventually she came out to loyal, roaring fans. Though late her performance did not disappoint.

That was the first time I had seen Janice perform on stage. The second was a few months later, on Labor Day at the New Orleans Pop Festival in Baton Rouge, Louisiana when she sang with her band Big Brother and the Holding Company. That performance was outstanding, one I will likely never forget. She appeared on the same stage as Santana, the Grateful Dead and Canned Heat. I attended this concert with my then boyfriend, a gentle fellow, who was also my roommate and one of my brother's chess partners. In fact, I met him through my brother. Six months later Janice was dead of an overdose at 27. Tragic.

When I left Harvard that summer, I was so revved that I bought a status symbol, a fabulous red Alfa-Romeo convertible that was used and cheap and made me feel so good jetting around New Orleans that it took the edge off of my not having a job. That car delivered status for nearly eight months until it needed a new engine.

Inspired by Harvard, I continued my interest in psychology by working at a local mental health hospital in New Orleans, where the director, true to the times, was conducting his own staffing experiment to learn what impact hiring non-nursing liberal arts graduates as "lay nurses" would have on the culture of the psych-unit and its patients. I was one.

Every morning at 7AM sharp, there was a nurses' report. One morning I learned that a young man who had been admitted for attempting suicide. Weeks had passed and he still wouldn't open up to his therapist. The therapist, a mild mannered man who would never have crossed boundaries even to save a patient, could do nothing with him. Nevertheless, when I used unconventional methods to put him under a sufficient pressure that he began talking in therapy, he was release in two weeks. But though successful, the methods were too radical for that supposedly progressive hospital. So I was laid off. Saved the patient, lost the job!

It was in this climate of rapid social change that I became an activist protesting the Vietnam war, supporting Black, women's, gay rights, abortion, protesting the banning of books and studying the rise of Maxist socialism. And it had all begun when I was 15 on a segregated New Orleans bus at the beginnings of integrated Rock and Roll dance music.

IV

A Philosophical Quest

A child's first philosophy usually begins with religion. This was certainly true for me. Father was baptized Catholic in the little fishing village of his birth, Igrane, Croatia before he immigrated to the USA with his mother to join her husband in the South Louisiana oyster fields. Once Father knew better, he quit the Catholic Church.

When Father married our mother, he joined her church. Therefore, my brother and I were baptized Lutheran and remained happily so for many years enjoying warm childhood friendships, games camping with neighbors and singing in the St. Mathew's Lutheran Church choir just blocks from our Gladiolus Street home. That church was our childhood country club. Unbeknownst to me, the twists and turns of life were to take me on a pilgrimage of discovering other worldviews.

Earthly love
philosophical intellect
  a complete life

With parents on public school teacher's salaries there was no money for advanced education but as luck would have it, in 1958 the public university system, Louisiana State University opened a branch in New Orleans (known as LSUNO). It was very inexpensive. The student body was small with only 200 students. The new faculty was composed of recent graduates recruited from some of the most prestigious Ivy League colleges in the country. From these newly graduated instructors we received a first class Ivy League education without the Ivy League price tag or having to leaving home.

For the first few years, there were just a few departments. Philosophy was one of them. When Dr. Daniel Anderson, a PhD. Graduate from Tulane University, accepted the appointment as Chairman of the new Philosophy Department, he selected twelve students from the freshmen class. I was one of them – why, I have no idea, as I was no academic. However, it may have been because I showed some youthful propensity for argument that he saw as trainable. I had, after all, inherited the fine art of questioning authority and being a contrarian from my immigrant military-gamesman father who loved the French art of repartee and verbal sparing.

That pile of books
unread thus far
   in living

It was Dr. Anderson, a Platonist, who introduced me to the fine art of philosophical questioning and my mother's death from cancer the year prior, which provided me with an easy leap from anger at God to questioning his existence. The study of western philosophy was the right fodder, which led me to agnosticism than to atheism.

Beginnings and endings
the river flows
   to the ocean

Andy, as he was known to his students, was a brilliant philosophy teacher but also a master of puns. It was not uncommon for him to run puns for 20 minutes while his students appropriately hissed, booed and yawned. Each student had a favorite form of humor. Tongue-in-cheek and droll humor were mine coupled with the occasional well-placed sarcastic witticism.

Whereas sarcasm can be readily recognized in a written text, tongue-in-cheek rarely can, as it is invisible, and an author's private chuckle which sneaks up on the unsuspecting reader, even educated ones, catching them unaware.

So dear readers beware, I carry on gleefully in Andy's honor!

Pining
for old pals
 the past is present

On his final trip to New Orleans, Andy and I enjoyed lunch at Fitzgerald's, a famous seafood restaurant on Lake Ponchartrain, sadly destroyed in 2005 when New Orleans levies broke and eighty percent of New Orleans flooded.

During lunch Andy gave me an original draft of his commentary on Plato's Symposium, The Mask of Dionysos. We shared stories of our LSUNO college days and spoke of many philosophical things. It was not until he returned home that I learned that he had cancer and was sure to die of it. Unbeknownst to me that lunch would be the last time I would eat at Fitzgerald's and it would be the last time that I would see my philosophical mentor and friend.

When will be the last time
you hear another's voice
the last phone call
the last look
last smile
last breath
when will that last time be

When some of Andy's students arranged a "Roasting Andy" Bon Voyage party, daydreaming that death would grant him a reprieve; I was too grieved to attend. But the week after the roasting I did call him. It took a few minutes for him to descend the staircase to the house phone, as grim reaper was rapidly approaching.

After reminding him that it was he who had directed me into Eastern philosophy, I felt duty bound to close the circle. But when I reported that ancient Taoist health philosophy believed that too much thinking could damage the digestive system, Andy's response was swift and sharpened to a Socratic point.

"I don't think that there can ever be too much thinking," he retorted.

A few months later Andy died. That telephone call was my bon voyage, his deathbed retort personifying the supremacy of his Socratic method. Like his venerated predecessor, Andy had died of the quintessential Western philosopher's disease. Perhaps he was a visionary. And perhaps considering the current dumped down education system and the rise of anti-intellectualism, he was right after all: there is no such thing as too much thinking.

Ask a question
get an answer
ask yet another question

After graduating, it was my good fortune to be admitted as a graduate student to the Department of Philosophy at the University of Pennsylvania. There were few females in the field of professional philosophy worldwide then which is still true today sixty years later. So for a southern female philosophy student in the USA to be accepted into a patriarchal Ivy League university was a worthy prize and validation of academic achievement.

As my father had no money for such a prestigious education, it was my godmother-aunt Marie, who in 1928 had put her younger sister, Doris, my mother through undergraduate college at Southeastern University when it first opened in their hometown, who now took up the gauntlet to do the same for me.

Even after becoming disenchanted with Wittgenstein, in the winter of 1963 I was fated to study even more linguistic analysis, this time at the University of Penn with Dr. Paul Ziff who's classes I found bloody boring coupled with the distasteful weather in his dark, dank, cold basement classroom in an old stone building. It seemed like a waste of my aunt's hard earned money. I didn't last the semester. When President John Kennedy was shot, I quit and returned to New Orleans.

A brief engagement to a male student in religious history had turned soar. And the thought of playing second fiddle as a wife was so repugnant that I just walked away. I thought I was returning to a former "passionate friendship" hoping to pick up where we left off. But alas, life had other plans.

More than a sister
less than a lover
once in a lifetime
thinking it would last forever -
how wrong I was

With very few female philosophers in the sexist patriarchal university system because of the subjugation of educated women, I was never able to get a university teaching position. We were not wanted. Ruth Bader Ginsberg born five years earlier had experienced the same doors closing in her face, as did every educated woman of the post World War II generation. Barred from university professorships, law firms, and discriminated against in hiring, educated women were told we were either too qualified or not qualified enough.

Out of the womb
full strident women
hammered by patriarchy - still
    standing tall

Remembering that Dr. Anderson had told me, "You may not be able to get a teaching post at a university but your education in philosophy has prepared you to think clearly and logically." That is by far a greater achievement, indeed.

Even in the 1980s, when I tried to enter a Masters of Fine Arts program, I was told I needed a "comprehensive body of work." For years I successfully operated a restoration and gliding art studio and developing a "comprehensive body of work." I applied to the Masters of Fine Arts program again in the mid 1980s. In a reverse discrimination move, the Chairman of the University of New Orleans (formerly LSUNO) art department told me my work "was too developed" and "left nothing for the university art adviser to teach" - the proverbial Catch 22.

Decades passed, three of them, I still felt that western philosophy was fundamentally deeply flawed but I had been unable to identify what those flaws were through the application of western logic alone, a fruitless circular endeavor indeed. It was Ludwig Wittgenstein who had placed the final nail in the coffin of Platonism calling all philosophical questions "nonsense" - and nonsense it all seemed.

The philosophy of the Orient had been lost to the west around 340AD with the burning of the Alexandra Library. Only fragments of what came before Plato had survived in its basement. Thinking of these early manuscripts as insignificant, subsequent centuries of western university philosophers minimized their contributions by labeling them "Pre-Socratics" as if nothing existing before Plato held any academic merit. Nonetheless, even these fragments led to discoveries.

East West North South
four dimensions
   searching for truth

So I turned to the Orient. No authoritative Eastern philosopher had been within my reach in mid-1970. Undeterred, my search for Eastern teachers continued. In those years these teachers were scarce. But as a visual artist and sculptor, hearing that the Japanese-American sculptor, Isamu Noguchi was living in New York City, hoping to work with him as he had with Brancusi, I wrote for an apprenticeship but sadly it was too late. At 76 he was not taking apprentices.

Not philosophy
but art
   lit a way

Determined to avoid my mother's fate of dying young from a fatal disease, my philosophical travels led to a study of every self-care practice and health preservation tradition I could find including ancient Asian food energetics, Japanese macrobiotic cooking and shiatsu, acupressure, self-massage, moxibustion, Indian yoga, Chinese qigong and later innovative mental health and still later its advance into a positive psychology movement.

As I studied all things Asian in the 1980s, I also began to teach what I was learning to try to help others improve their health. Often, I found it difficult to accept that lessons alone did not motivate students. Understandably though, after all, it was my fate and my great good fortune to have had a mother who died at a young age, showing me the way and giving me the necessary motivation to continue undaunted.

Daughter's life long
raison d'être
   always - Mother

An opportunity arose from an unusual post World War II health practice originating in Japan with George and Lima Ohsawa, which they named "macrobiotics," arriving in the U.S. in 1965. In mid-1980, when a Kushi Institute trained teacher arrived in New Orleans, that was my entry point.

On one of many trips to in San Francisco, I mentioned to a friend that I had been experiencing some fatigue though not feeling ill otherwise. She told me she had heard of a Macrobiotic teacher in New Orleans. I had heard the term "Macrobiotics" only once before as early as 1966 while at lunch with a university colleague at Five Happiness Chinese Restaurant in New Orleans. Knowing of my determination to avoid my mother's fate, this colleague had told me that some Japanese teachers now in the US were teaching how to use food to reverse cancer. That comment stuck and twenty years later it surfaced.

Oriental philosophy had migrated only recently to the USA and then only to the West Coast. Indian yoga was the first to arrive followed by the Zen philosophy introduced at Berkeley by Dr. Alan Watts and also the qi-dance of Chungliang "Al" Huang. Finally in 1976 Esalen Institute opened its doors for laypersons.

And on a visit to California in 1996, I wandered into The East West Bookstore in downtown Mt. View where Dr. Huston Smith was speaking. Dr. Smith, a scholar and practitioner of comparative religions, author of <u>The World's Religions</u> was no stranger to me. I had previously seen Bill Moyers' interviews of him in a PBS four part series.

That evening I walked the three blocks over to the bookstore to hear Dr. Smith and bought his book. When he signed my book he invited me to attend his seminar at Esalen Institute. So in the spring of 2003, I made my way to Esalen to attend his workshop titled "Applied Wisdom." This was the door to a new world that I had been seeking.

During his talk about God, Dr. Smith, who he always seemed to be seeking, something he said prompted me to quote a fragment from a early Greek philosopher regarding the "Fallacy of Composition." Smith did not think that my reference was accurate but after his break, he returned to say that yes indeed I had been correct. It was then that Smith urged us all to come back to Esalen to meet Dr. Peter Kingsley, a philosophy trained Cambridge scholar who had for years studied the ancient early Greeks, was to co-chair his upcoming workshop in 2004.

Caged within one's time
happenstance frees us
   great good fortune

So in March of that year, I returned to meet Dr. Kingsley, author and Pre-Socratic scholar who, like myself, had come to understand something of grave importance was missing in the Western philosophical tradition.

When Kingsley commented that Western philosophy had "not been written correctly" and that "Western culture lives in a myth," I finally felt that I was in the right room. He continued by saying: "at the root of Western culture 2500 years ago is a lost sacred tradition." It was this Western spiritual tradition that Kingsley had discovered and which he had devoted his life to reviving.

History turns on a dime
centuries between
   fresh truths

Learning of Dr. Kingsley's extraordinary discovery, I now had authoritarian scholastic verification of a missing historical piece. He had uncovered rare manuscripts about the earlier Greek, Priest of Apollo, and philosopher-poet, Parmenides. Parmenides had been buried deep in Greek pre-history and Plato, writing his own historical legacy had commandeered Parmenides for his own purposes. Kingsley verified that what I had been taught as western philosophy had been based on Plato's self-serving lie.

While on the main road
a detour
 took me to it

In the centuries since Plato, western philosophers taught standards that one could reason one's way to the "good life." Western philosophy is analytic focused on the traditional polar opposites of Aristotle. Plato truncated the early ancient Greeks concept of *logique* and its original meaning had been completely lost to the West.

Based solely on Plato's truncated reporting; western logic now emphasizes rational reasoning. Western logic is linear while that of the East is circular. In the East, natural inner knowing arises with non-thinking serenity.

The goal of Eastern practices has been to turn thinking off and activate inner tranquility without interference from the busy, thinking mind. Eastern Greek philosophy understood life as so much wider than mere dry intellectual reasoning.

East to West
the bird of wisdom carried
   a twig of truth

Oriental health preservation practices are "applied" philosophy unlike the purely analytical cognitive approach of western philosophy and its sciences. There is a crucial difference between the two. The goal of early Greek and eastern philosophy, as Dr. Kingsley puts it, is to "come to the point that we just experience" while the goal of western philosophy is knowledge of methods and the application of Aristotelian logic. The difference is crucial. The Fallacy of Composition states that once a whole is divided, it can never be reunited - sort of a Humpty Dumpty theory. Similarly, Joseph Campbell was known for saying that as along as we all agree on one God, there is unity and peace but once divided there is war.

Ancient Taoism from Dynastic pre-China brought to the west the secret of a happy, healthy long life and peace of mind. To achieve inner peace and mental clarity, Taoism taught that the busy thinking mind, the cognitive mind must be out of the way in order to bring about stillness and insight which is what the early Greeks before Plato meant by logic. Once in a safe, quiet present, relaxation restores us to our natural state, that of inner peace.

Dr. Kingsley had discovered this Eastern link, finding that those labeled "Pre-Socratics"... "weren't theoretical or speculative and nothing like rationalists." Through his discoveries Dr. Kingsley finally reunited the East and West in a way it may have once existed in the Mediterranean.
The two halves became one - again.

~

I have lived many lives in this one
What's next -
Repeat please

Epilogue

Watching her child in the living room of our cottage putting on a 78 RPM, winding up the Victrola and twirling to Strauss waltzes, Mother sent me to dance lessons where I learned every dance from ballet to jitterbug.

Today I saw British actress, Lily James in Cinderella - so inspired was I, that I would change my age and my name on the chance that I could be her just once to relive the cinematic 1950s life with my Aunt-godmother Marie sewing all my ball gowns which she cleverly copied from Hollywood movie sets.

Had it not been for the emergence of Rock and Roll in New Orleans in 1954, my life would have been lesser indeed. Less colorful, less passionate, less connected to my beloved New Orleans. For it was New Orleans born Rock and Roll and the Black musicians of New Orleans who influenced my political awareness and connected me to the Black civil rights movement inspiring my own political activism of the 1970s.

Surrounded by art, music and games
dance and fencing could have been my fate
yet artist-to-writer became my trek
and the rhythm of words and phrases, my thrill -
Oh, destiny, what self will I become now

~

ACKNOWLEDGEMENTS

Special thanks to Karen E. Doby of Dancing Shark Studio for her indispensible technical support with cover and copy editing. And to my kvetch sounding board members: Bobbie Geary, Gloria Daniels, Carolyn W. Levy, and Lee Meitzen Grue.

PHYLLIS PARUN
Poet - Author

Phyllis Parun is a deeply honest author and a quintessential example of Cocteau's dictum that *"writing should be an act of love otherwise its nothing but handwriting."*

Born in the mysterious city of New Orleans, Parun is a self-styled creative with an individual intelligence whose voyage of self-discovery destined her to develop first as a visual artist then as a gilding craftswoman and a pioneer community *culture*r finally as philosophical poet. As a writer she has explored many literary forms: non-fiction, essays on healthy life, short stories, philosophical and poetic memoir. Community activism set her course of involvement in black, gay and women's rights and in the arts of the 1970s then in the healing arts of the 1980s-90s. This is an author who writes with insight and honesty about the human life as she has experienced it.

New Orleans Born her poetic homage to the influences of her childhood family and her city of New Orleans while **New Orleans Between Poetry and the Blues** meanders to the year 2000 sometimes with scathing humor. **My Dance With Time** features stories from seven decades about the people, eras, and events that shaped her through many personal tales, which take the reader on a deep journey into their own long forgotten memories.

Ms. Parun's published genres include interviews, articles, essays, poems, e-Zines, visual art, and photography in a wide variety of local and national publications. The Beachcomber (LSUNO, 1961-63), AOBTA Pulse (2006), American Assn. of Oriental Medicine (1995), Macrobiotics Today (1991-2015), Gulf Coast Arts Review (2004), ArtLit (2006), Iris (2005), Qi: Journal of Traditional Eastern Health and Fitness (1995), The New Laurel Review (2001- 2015), The Maple Leaf Rag III (2006), <u>Mending for Memory</u> (2017) and creator of "The New Orleans Living Treasurers Award" and her self published e-zine: "The New Orleans Avant-Garde" (2008 ongoing).

Ms. Parun is also an accomplished visual artist with many local exhibits to her credit, her special talent excelled in the gilded arts in panel painting and glass gilding.

End Notes

Thank you for reading

**Sign up for
author newsletter and
new releases**

pbpstudio@yahoo.com

Published Titles

New Orleans Born (2019)
***New Orleans Between Poetry
and the Blues (2019)***
Love's Arrows (an EBook)
My Dance with Time (2022)

Order direct from
www.PHYLLISPARUN.com
"BOOKS FOR SALE"

Also available at
Your local bookstores,
Barnes & Noble,
Kobe, Amazon Kindle,
Goodreads, Walmart
Ingram Spark

REVIEWS WELCOMED
On Kindle at
Amazon USA
https://www.amazon.com/-/e/B006HX9348

NOTES

NOTES

NOTES

www.ingramcontent.com/pod-product-compliance
Lightning Source LLC
Chambersburg PA
CBHW052207090526
44583CB00017BA/2409